You Don't Have to Be *WRONG* to *REPENT!*

Craig Hill

You Don't Have to Be Wrong to Repent!
Copyright © 1987 Craig S. Hill

Family Foundations International
P.O. Box 320
Littleton, Colorado 80160

Printed in the United States of America

All scripture quotations, not otherwise noted, appear in The New American Standard Bible. The following versions have also been used: *The New American Standard Bible*, The Lockman Foundation, 1960, 1962, 1963, 1968, 1971, 1973, 1975; *King James Version*, Thomas Nelson, Inc., Publishers; *The Amplified Bible*, Zondervan Bible Publishers, 1965, 12ᵗʰ Printing, 1975.

First Printing 1987
Second Printing 1995
Third Printing 1996
Fourth Printing 2000
Fifth Printing 2004

Craig Hill, along with his wife Jan and their two sons, live in Denver, Colorado, where Craig and Jan give senior leadership to Family Foundations International, the ministry through which life-changing seminars are conducted throughout the world.

God has given Craig unique insight into marriage, family and interpersonal relationships, resulting in his ability to identify for many people root causes of relational conflict, compulsive habits, low self-esteem, work-aholism and undesirable life patterns which are repeated from one generation to the next.

By interweaving personal stories with biblical truth, God has anointed Craig to pierce through the veil of the mind to minister to the depths of the heart, resulting in real life change for many.

For a free catalog of other materials by
Craig Hill please write to:

**Family Foundations International
P.O. Box 320
Littleton, Colorado 80160**

YOU DON'T HAVE TO BE
WRONG TO REPENT

"You don't have to be wrong to repent."

That was the phrase that the Lord spoke to me one day as I sat in a restaurant with my family, attempting to get my four-year old son to eat his hamburger. Joshua and I had come to an irreconcilable standoff regarding the hamburger. We had gone to the restaurant after church on a Sunday, and he had wanted a hamburger for lunch. However, when the meal came, I noticed that the hamburger was much too big for Joshua to eat without it being cut. So, I simply reached over with my knife and fork and cut his hamburger in half.

I then said, "There, now it will be much easier for you to eat." Joshua looked at me with an anguished look of shock and disbelief and replied with tears starting to roll out of his eyes, "You ruined it! I'm not going to eat it!" I tried for several minutes to convince him that the hamburger would taste just the same whether it was cut or not. However, he still refused and demanded that I put it back together, or at least get him a new hamburger.

Since neither bribery nor threats seemed to motivate Joshua to stop crying and eat, it suddenly dawned on me to pray and ask the Lord how to solve the problem.

As I consulted my Father regarding the matter, he spoke into my spirit that I should repent and ask my son's forgiveness. I thought to myself, "What should I repent of? I'm right. I can't repent if I'm the one who's

1

right. He should eat his hamburger, and I was right to cut it, because it was too big for him to handle."

Then the Holy Spirit spoke to me something like the following: "You are right about the superficial issue of the hamburger, but *you don't have to be wrong to repent*. The hamburger is not really the issue of concern at all, but the message conveyed to your son through your method and attitude is of great concern. Joshua is not reacting concerning the hamburger at all, but rather is reacting to a message you conveyed to him through your actions and attitude regarding his identity and value as a person. In this you are wrong and need to repent. But you have been so focused on the external issue (the hamburger) that you haven't seen the real problem."

I was beginning to see something, so I asked the Lord for more clarification. The Holy Spirit continued speaking into my spirit: "When you reached over and cut the food on Joshua's plate, you didn't extend to him the courtesy of communicating with him your intentions before just treating his plate as your own. Then when he reacted, you continued to treat him as if he were the one with an attitude problem and didn't acknowledge his feelings on the matter at all. You treated him as if he had no feelings or as if his feelings didn't matter. How would you like it if someone uninvited reached over to your plate and began to tinker with your food?"

"The message you sent to Joshua in acting without consulting him was, "You are not really of any value. Your opinion doesn't really count. You're just a child, and I'm an adult. I can treat you however I please, and I don't need to consider your opinion or feelings. You have no right to make decisions, because you have no wisdom and are of no value."

"Then as you persisted in your position that you are right, and he needs to stop the commotion and eat, you have sent him the message that you don't care about him and that the issue (the hamburger) is really more important to you than he is a person. Through all this, you have sent to your son a message that you are arbitrary, uncaring and authoritarian and that in your sight, he is worthless, not worthy of even having charge over his own plate of food, incapable of making any decision, and nothing but a bother to you."

I finally saw that although I had been right on the external issue, I had conveyed to my little son a devastating and destructive message through my blindness to his feelings and my focus on the external issue. All that time I had thought that we were talking about a hamburger, while in actuality; we were discussing Joshua's value as a person.

The Lord spoke all this to me in just a few quick seconds. I decided to check it out by asking Joshua if this were true. So I asked, "Joshua, have I made you feel like you're not very important to me?" His countenance suddenly changed, and he began to look at me as if maybe, somehow I really did understand, and answered, "Yes." I continued, "Did you feel that Daddy got in your space without asking first?" "Yes," he exclaimed. I then said, "Joshua, I'm sorry. I can now see that I was very wrong to treat you that way. I should have talked to you before I cut your food. Will you forgive me?" He replied "Yes, Daddy." I continued, "I made you feel that eating the hamburger was more important to me than you are. That is not at all true. I love you very much. You are more important to me than the issue of whether you eat this hamburger or not. I was wrong to talk to you that way. Will you forgive me?" "Yes, Daddy," he responded. I then offered to buy Josh a new hamburger, since I had in fact violated his personal identity and removed his choice regarding the first one. However, now that the identity problem was solved, he thought that the hamburger on his plate would be just fine, and it really was much easier to eat cut in half. As soon as the problem regarding his value as a person was solved, the problem with the hamburger went away.

Very often couples have come into my office for ministry, at odds with one another over various issues. When I have suggested to either partner that he/she repent and ask his/her partner's forgiveness, he/she finds it impossible to do because he/she is convinced that he/she is right and therefore cannot repent. Since each partner is convinced that he/she is right, neither can repent, so the relationship remains broken and the dispute unresolved. As long as the eyes of both partners remain focused on the external issue, they will both continue to believe that they are right, not realizing that you don't have to be wrong (regarding the issue) to repent.

It is the devil's purpose to see that neither partner in a marriage ever sees messages sent and communication taking place on the relational level. If the enemy can sow relational patterns in our lives, by which we destroy ourselves and our own relationships, then he has very little work to do in order to accomplish his purposes in our lives.

SCHEMES OF THE DEVIL

"Finally, be strong in the Lord, and in the strength of His might. Put on the full armor of God, that you may be able to stand firm against the schemes of the devil. For our struggle is not against flesh and blood, but against the rulers, against the powers, against the world forces of this darkness, against the spiritual forces of wickedness in heavenly places."
(Ephesians 6:10-12)

The devil has specific schemes through which he works. They are well thought-out plans devised to deceive and destroy you if you don't gain knowledge that a specific scheme is operating in your life. Let us now look at two specific schemes that the devil often uses in the lives of married couples. These are lies in which we believe and trust.

1) "When a disagreement begins, my problem is really my husband/wife." Ephesians 6:12 tells us that the struggle is not against flesh and blood. But the first lie we often get drawn into believing is that the struggle really is against this other flesh and blood person. We then spend our time and energy battling

with each other, and the rulers and powers and spiritual forces of wickedness in heavenly places laugh at us.

When we, as husbands and wives, are in disagreement with each other, we block the Father from working through us.

"Again I say to you, that if two of you agree on earth about anything that they may ask, it shall be done for them by My Father Who is in heaven."
(Matthew 18:19)

Obviously, the converse is also true. "If any two of you disagree about anything that they may ask, it shall not be done for them by my Father Who is in heaven." So you can see that the Father in heaven is blocked from moving on your behalf often due to disagreement in your marriage. I believe that it is a prime objective of the devil to keep a husband and wife at all costs from coming into agreement with each other. He knows that when you as a couple come into agreement and you pray, you release the Father in heaven to do what you have prayed.

The truth of the matter is that when you are in the midst of a dispute with your marriage partner, that your partner is not your enemy, but, instead, you have both simply fallen right into a well-planned, premeditated scheme of the devil. When you first sense in your heart irritation toward your partner, it's time to stop talking and ask the Holy Spirit to give you revelation of the scheme of the devil that is beginning to work.

2) "I'm right about this issue, and my partner is wrong and needs to change." The deception here is that you may be actually right about the issue, but the real discussion is not about the issue. There are two levels of communication. The first is on the level of the external issue about which you think you are talking. The second is on the level of the personal identity. Most of the time, when a dispute arises between a husband and wife, the real discussion is on the level of the identity. If neither of them realizes this, they may spend hours or even days discussing an irrelevant issue, (such as I began to do with my son about his hamburger) deeply hurting each other in the process, and in the end never resolving the dispute.

CURSING MY PARTNER'S IDENTITY

This second scheme of the devil works through what I call cursing the identity. Your identity is that part of you through which you perceive who you are. Every person has a deep need to perceive himself as valuable. The primary aspect of blessing has to do with honor. Cursing has to do with the impartation of worthlessness and lack of value. On the external level of communication, you may be right regarding an issue, while on the relational level you are unwittingly cursing your spouse's identity. In this case, you need to repent and ask your partner's forgiveness. Once you have cursed your partner's identity, whether intentional or not, the discussion is no longer about the issue. It is now a discussion of the value of each person to each other. If you ask the Lord to make you sensitive, you can tell almost immediately when you have cursed your partner's identity. You will see an emotional reaction of some type.

In his book *"The Marriage Builder,"*[i] Dr. Lawrence Crabb states that there are two basic longings inside a person in the realm of the identity. These are: 1) Security and 2) Significance. Dr. Crabb defines these as follows: "Security: a convinced awareness of being unconditionally and totally loved without needing to change in order to win love, loved by a love that is freely given, that cannot be earned and therefore cannot be lost." "Significance: a realization that I am engaged in a responsibility or job that is truly important, whose results will not evaporate with time, but will last through eternity, that fundamentally involves having a meaningful impact on another person, a job for which I am completely adequate."

Dr. Crabb also discusses the fact that although both security and significance are important for both marriage partners, the deeper need of the wife is usually in the realm of security and the deeper need of the husband in the realm of significance. In other words, a wife will usually tend to perceive herself as valuable if she feels secure in the love of her husband. A husband will usually tend to feel valuable if he is engaged in some significant activity or task.

A husband primarily conveys love to his wife through sending her a message on the relational level of

---

[i] Lawrence J. Crabb, Jr. *The Marriage Builder* (Grand Rapids: Zondervan, 1982) pp. 80 - 81

communication that she as a person is valuable to him, that she is a priority to him above other activities. She must know that her opinions, her feelings, and her words are important to him. A wife, on the other hand, primarily conveys love to her husband through sending him a message on the relational level that he is adequate as a husband, that he is a good provider, and an important person to her. He must know that he is significant and respected in her eyes.

So, you can quickly see that a husband can deeply wound and curse the identity of his wife most easily by sending her a relational message that she means nothing to him and that she is very low or non-existent on his priority list. A wife can most easily curse her husband's identity by sending him a relational message that he is inadequate as a husband, father, provider, and a man.

Cursing the identity of a marriage partner can be used intentionally as a weapon to wound when you have bought into the lie that your partner is your enemy. Most often, however quarrels and arguments start when one partner through his/her words, actions or attitudes inadvertently curses the identity of the other. Very frequently you may curse your partner's identity without knowing it, just as I did to my little four-year old son.

Let me give you a couple of examples. Bill had a need to travel out of town on business one week. Since his business would conclude on Thursday, he decided it would be a great idea to fly his wife, Sue, out to meet him and spend a three-day weekend together in that city. Bill had rented a car for the week for his business, but had found that he could get a much cheaper one for the weekend for their own personal use. He planned to rent the cheaper car at the airport when Sue arrived and have her follow him back to the hotel to turn in the more expensive car. Both Bill and Sue were really looking forward to a nice, romantic weekend together.

When Sue arrived at the airport, Bill explained the car situation to her, and she was happy to follow him back to the hotel in the cheaper car. Bill waited for Sue to start her car, and when he saw that she had, he started for the hotel. However, Sue could not figure out how to get the parking brake released so she could drive, and Bill was already driving off. Bill was used to traveling out of town and jumping in any old rental car and driving off. However, Sue rarely traveled out of town and rarely drove any other car than her own. Finally, she got the brake released and got out of the parking lot with Bill just barely in sight.

Bill accelerated at the entrance ramp to the freeway headed for the hotel. Once on the freeway, he moved over to the left lane and took off like a bullet, or at least so it seemed to Sue. She was not yet used to the car she was driving and felt like she was endangering her life to follow him at such speed. However, it was dark and she was losing his taillights amidst other cars. She wasn't familiar with that city and had no idea where the hotel was. Just as she caught sight of Bill's taillights again, Sue saw him dart across two lanes of traffic and exit the freeway. Almost causing an accident in her attempt to move into the right lane to follow her husband, and being honked at by another driver, Sue exited the freeway and finally arrived at the hotel. By this time she was furious with Bill.

As Bill opened the car door to help her out, Sue glowered at him and said, "Why didn't you wait for me? Why do you have to drive like you're on your way to a fire, when we're supposed to be enjoying a relaxing weekend together? I was almost killed trying to follow you. Don't you ever think about me at all?"

Of course, this was all big news to Bill. He was greatly surprised and hurt to be greeted in such a way at the hotel by Sue. Bill then replied, "I did wait for you. I could see you behind me in my rear view mirror all the way. And, anyway, I had to speed up on the freeway in order to fit into the flow of traffic. I'm sorry you had a problem following me. Anyway, we're here now, so let's forget it."

But Sue wasn't satisfied, and she didn't forget it. She was still furious, and Bill didn't seem to think that there was even a problem. Bill, on the other hand, thought that he had apologized and that it was an insignificant event. When Sue began to question Bill again about why he didn't wait for her, he once again explained and defended his driving. By this time, he was thinking, "Why did I ever invite her out here this weekend? It's much cheaper to just stay at home and argue. Who needs this?"

To make a long story shorter, Bill and Sue spent the entire evening arguing about Bill's driving habits. They allowed the scheme of the devil to ruin their entire weekend and significantly damage their marriage relationship. Neither of them recognized that from the very start, they were not discussing Bill's driving. They were really discussing Sue's value to Bill and then Bill's adequacy as a husband.

Inadvertently, by driving the way he had, Bill had sent to Sue a relational message that he didn't really care about her as a person. His goal of driving to the hotel was more important to him than she was as a person. She was feeling that he was inconsiderate and didn't care if he lost her on the freeway. Because Bill never understood that he had inadvertently cursed his wife's identity, it didn't make any sense to him when she accused him that evening of not loving her or caring for her. He replied, "Why do you think I set aside the time and spent the money to fly you out here for the weekend – because I don't love you or care about you?"

When Sue had initially accused Bill of not waiting for her, she was cursing his identity and accusing him of not being an adequate husband to her. By her not repenting of cursing his identity, she continued to send to Bill a relational message that he was inadequate and totally displeasing to her. All he could think was that there was no way to please his wife. He spends a lot of extra money to fly her out of town to spend a romantic weekend with him, and all she can do is complain about some small insignificant detail and accuse him, so he thinks.

By Bill's not repenting of cursing his wife's identity, he continued to send her a relational message that he really didn't care, and that she was not valuable to him. She kept thinking, "How could I have married such an insensitive, uncaring, and blind person?"

Both Bill and Sue were kept from repenting and solving the problem, because they both continued to focus on the external issues and were each convinced that he/she was right. Bill could have easily settled the dispute and restored the relationship by asking a couple of simple questions of the Lord when Sue attacked him. "Lord, have I cursed her identity in some way?" Then, after hearing from God, "How have I done so?" Next, he could have said to his wife, after gaining understanding from the Lord, "Honey, by driving the way I did, did I cause you to feel as if I don't really care very much for you?" When Sue responded affirmatively, he then could have said, "I'm so sorry for making you feel that way. I was insensitive to you and didn't realize it. I love you so much and had no intention to make you feel unloved. Will you forgive me?"

Had Bill done this, he and his wife could have spent a wonderful weekend together and enjoyed each other's presence, instead of spending the weekend arguing and letting the scheme of the devil destroy their relationship.

Let's consider one more example. Cathy had been praying for her husband, Joe, for a couple of years. Joe had committed his life to the Lord several years ago, but had never really grown spiritually or had any great interest in spiritual things. Cathy, on the other hand had grown tremendously in the last couple of years. Since her children were in school during the day and she didn't work, she had a fair amount of time to pursue spiritual things. Cathy listened to Christian radio most of the day while working around her house and was able to spend a couple of hours in Bible study and prayer almost every day after the kids left for school. She also attended a women's Bible study once a week, a home fellowship group, and church a couple of times a week.

Joe's job as an attorney kept him very busy. He was frequently required to travel out of town and often had to work late into the evening. Cathy had been praying that Joe would get as excited about and committed to the Lord as she was. She wanted him to really become the spiritual head of the home. Frequently, she left interesting cassette tapes for him to hear in his car on the way to work, but he rarely listened to them.

One weekend Cathy convinced Joe to try studying the Bible and praying with her for just ten minutes each morning before work. She was so excited when he agreed. Cathy called up several of her friends on the phone and asked them to pray for Joe on Monday morning.

Cathy was bubbling over with excitement as she and Joe sat down to read the Bible Monday morning. "Well, what part would you like to read," she inquired? "I don't know," Joe answered. So Cathy suggested the book that she had been studying in the women's Bible study. Joe agreed. They opened up their Bibles and read the first chapter. Cathy then asked Joe to comment on what the Lord was speaking to him through the passage. Joe was feeling a little uncomfortable, because he was really out of his field and wasn't exactly sure what it meant to have the Lord speak, anyway. He mentioned a couple of things that he saw in the passage. Cathy, in her zeal to expose to Joe the richness and depth of the Scriptures, then proceeded to expound upon the passage for about ten minutes. Joe was silent.

She then said, "Let's pray now." Joe agreed. Joe had always felt a little uncomfortable praying out loud, but he went ahead and awkwardly muttered a couple sentences asking for wisdom and praying for God's blessing for the day. Cathy then entered into His presence, bound the devil, spoke the Word, released the power, and went around the world a couple of times in prayer, all in Jesus' name. When she finished, Joe said he was in a hurry and quickly left for work.

The next morning Joe said that he couldn't pray with her, because he had to be at the office a little early. He continued to make excuses not to meet with her again for prayer and Bible study. Cathy was once again disappointed and hurt that Joe just wasn't interested in spiritual things.

What Cathy had failed to realize was that she had inadvertently cursed her husband's identity. Her goal was to interest him in spiritual things and to help him assume a role of spiritual leadership in the home.

But, instead, through her insensitivity to her husband's need to feel significant and adequate as a husband, Cathy had cursed his identity and caused him to feel inadequate and of no spiritual value inside.

When women are hurt inside and have had their identities cursed by their husbands, usually they will express that in some way to their husbands. However, often when a husband is hurt and has had his identity cursed by his wife, he won't express that, but will rather withdraw from the relationship and just be silent. That is what Joe did. Cathy didn't understand Joe's reaction and interpreted it as Joe's having no interest in spiritual matters. Actually, Joe had a great interest in spiritual things, but was threatened by Cathy's superior knowledge of the Bible and practice in the language of prayer. Without knowing it, Cathy was constantly cursing Joe's identity and he felt like a spiritual dummy. There was no way he could compete with her spirituality, and it deeply hurt him to be made to feel so inadequate, so he simply wouldn't participate with his wife in spiritual things.

The more Cathy tried to get Joe to hear this tape, or read that book or go to this meeting, the more she unwittingly drove him away from the Lord. Cathy could have easily resolved their relationship and drawn Joe closer to the Lord if she would have recognized how she was cursing his identity.

When Joe got very quiet, and began to withdraw from her, Cathy could have asked the Lord if she had cursed her husband's identity. Then she could have asked the Lord how she did so. When she had revelation from God, she could have then asked Joe, "Have I made you feel as though Bible study and praying are more important to me than you are as a person to me? Have I made you feel that you are very displeasing to me and not acceptable to me as my husband?" When he answers affirmatively, she could then say, "I had no idea that I was not honoring you as the precious husband that you are. I am so grateful to God for giving you to me as a gift. I've been wrong in my attitude toward you in not honoring you as my husband and in making you feel unacceptable in my sight, and in not being grateful to God for giving you to me as my husband. Will you forgive me?"

Had Cathy done this, she could have begun to melt the hardness in her husband's heart and restore their relationship together. She would have released her husband to truly pursue his role as the spiritual head of his home, secure in the love and honor of his wife, without his personal identity being at stake. However, Cathy had not repented and asked her husband's forgiveness because she was convinced that she was right on the issue. She thought that the problem was that her husband was just unspiritual and didn't want to know the Lord. She was convinced that she was right and needed no repentance, but that he was the one who needed to repent and change. She was blind to her own sin of pride and of dishonoring her husband and constantly, through her attitude, cursing his identity. Remember, you don't have to be wrong (on the issue) to repent.

RESOLVING RELATIONAL CONFLICT

Conflicts within a marriage and almost any other type of relationship usually have to do with identity cursing. The following simple steps are designed to help you quickly resolve conflicts and draw closer to each other and to the Lord.

1) Ask the Lord to make you sensitive to your marriage partner to discern when you have hurt him/her. Anger, defensiveness, coldness, pouting, or withdrawal are sure indicators of the cursing of your partner's identity.

2) If your partner has attacked or hurt you, go to the Lord, confess your hurt, and let the Lord be your source of comfort and peace. Then forgive your partner. Totally release and hold him/her accountable no longer.

3) When you have discerned that your partner is hurt, don't argue and defend your point. Often times it takes only a split second to get revelation from the Lord as to what the real issue is and how to deal with it. Ask the Lord two simple questions: "How have I cursed my partner's identity?" and "How have I made him/her feel?"

4) Verify with your partner how he/she feels. Feelings usually convey what has happened in the realm of the identity.   You may ask, "How have I made you feel? Sometimes your partner may be too hurt to tell you and will claim that he/she is not hurt or simply will not speak. But usually he/she will tell you

what the feeling is. If not, then you must simply rely on the revelation of the Holy Spirit.

5) If your partner has shared with you the feeling, make sure that you have listened carefully and attentively and do not do any of these six things.[ii]

- Defend or explain your actions or words.
- Apologize tritely.
- Attack or tell how he/she hurt you, too.
- Say, "You shouldn't feel that way."
- Give advice.
- Give correction.

All six of these are ways that you can reject your partner and further curse his/her identity. Instead, acknowledge that you understand the feeling by repeating it to your partner, saying something such as, "So you feel like I don't really care about you?" or "You feel that no matter what you do, you can never please me?"

6) Repent and ask your spouse to forgive you for cursing his/her identity. In doing so, do not discuss the problem. Do not justify, explain or say, "If I was wrong." Say something such as: "I've been blind. I didn't know that I made you feel _____.
God has convicted me that I was wrong. I have preferred myself above you. I'm so sorry for hurting you. Will you forgive me?" Inside each of us is a balance scale through which we offset any guilt we feel with blame against another person. When your spouse

---

[ii] Lawrence J. Crabb, Jr. *The Marriage Builder* (Grand Rapids: Zondervan, 1982) pp. 80 - 81

curses your identity and hurts you, if you don't immediately go to the Lord and receive His love and forgive your spouse, you will have resentment and bitterness grow up inside you. Although we don't like to think of it this way, resentment and bitterness are really just more acceptable words for hatred. Hatred is sin. When you are in sin, you feel guilty. Guilt is a tormenting emotion with which we cannot continue to lie without doing something to quench it. So guilt is often offset, and hatred is justified by magnifying blame against the offending party. If you concentrate on the wrong done to you by your partner, and blame and accuse him/her in your heart, you can justify to yourself your own sin of hatred and bitterness. Thus you balance off your own guilt with blame toward an offending party.

If you are the offending partner, or an argument has already begun over a particular issue, undoubtedly your partner has done the same thing and has offset the guilt for his/her own sin with blame toward you. When you humble yourself, repent and ask forgiveness, you are emptying the blame side of your partner's balance scale. You are asking him/her to empty the blame side of the account. Your partner is then left with a full dish on the guilt side. Usually, your partner will then also repent and ask you to forgive him/her for a wrong attitude. In this way, both of you have emptied both sides of the scale, and you are once again free.

However, sometimes (not often) your partner may not be willing to forgive you. This is usually because both sides of the scale are piled very high with guilt and blame. There may be great fear of experiencing the mountain of unresolved guilt if the mountain of blame is removed. In this case, just continue on in a repentant attitude and pray for your partner for him/her to be able to receive enough of God's love to remove the fear and forgive you. You're not responsible for your partner's response. But your part is to: A) unconditionally forgive your partner, B) repent of your sin, C) ask your partner's forgiveness and D) trust God as your source for the results.

7) Bless your marriage partner. After you have asked forgiveness for cursing your partner's identity, bless him/her. You do so by conveying to him/her words of value and honor. You may say something such as: "I love you so much. You are very special to me. You are a blessing from the Lord." Ask the Lord to give you creative ways to bless your partner, and make him/her feel special, important, and honored by you.

If you will follow these seven points, not as a formula, but as guidelines, and let the Holy Spirit make you sensitive to the cursing and blessing of your partner's identity, you will walk in a blessed marriage relationship. Your partner truly will become to you a source of blessing and joy rather than of hurt and unhappiness. Remember in any argument or conflict, regarding the disputed issue, **YOU DON'T HAVE TO BE WRONG TO REPENT!**

I'M A NEW CREATION?

"Therefore, if anyone is in Christ, he is a new creation; old things have passed away: behold, all things have become new."

(II Corinthians 5:17 NKJV)

Craig Hill

Family Foundations International
P.O. Box 320
Littleton, Colorado 80160

Printed in the United States of America

Unless otherwise indicated, all Scripture quotations are taken from the New American Standard Bible (copyrighted 1985 by Thomas Nelson, Inc.)

NKJV indicates use of the New King James version, (copyrighted 1982 by Thomas Nelson, Inc.)

First Printing 1987
Second Printing 1995
Third Printing 1996
Fourth Printing 2000
Fifth Printing 2004

Craig Hill, along with his wife Jan and their two sons, live in Denver, Colorado, where Craig and Jan give senior leadership to Family Foundations International, the ministry through which life-changing seminars are conducted throughout the world.

God has given Craig unique insight into marriage, family and interpersonal relationships, resulting in his ability to identify for many people root causes of relational conflict, compulsive habits, low self-esteem, work-aholism and undesirable life patterns which are repeated from one generation to the next.

By interweaving personal stories with biblical truth, God has anointed Craig to pierce through the veil of the mind to minister to the depths of the heart, resulting in real life change for many.

For a free catalog of other materials by
Craig Hill please write to:

Family Foundations International
P.O. Box 320
Littleton, Colorado 80160

I'M A NEW CREATION?

"Therefore, if anyone is in Christ, he is a new creation; old things have passed away: behold, all things have become new." (II Corinthians 5:17 NKJV)

For most of us, many of these "old things" – the sinful attitudes and behaviors that dominate certain areas of our life – have not "passed away." Even after we have been born again and committed our lives to God, they continue to plague us. Because God's Word is true, it is unthinkable that this scripture is wrong. So we conclude that the problem is with us, we aren't good enough Christians, we do not have enough faith, or we aren't praying and studying the Bible enough!

Thus, scripture, which should elevate us in faith, becomes a condemnation to us. We consign ourselves to the outer fringe of Christian practice because we know in our heart that we don't attain its standards. Yet, this scripture and many others suggest we can live absolutely victorious lives. So, we are in a dilemma!

The answer is found in allowing the Word to divide between soul and spirit.

"For the word of God is living and active and sharper than any two-edged sword, and piercing as far as the division of soul and spirit, of both joints and marrow, and able to judge the thoughts and intentions of the heart." (Hebrews 4:12)

At conversion, your spirit passes from death to life. It is purged of the former corrupt nature of sin and totally filled with the nature of Jesus Christ. This is true of all Christians, no matter how sin-entangled they become. This sinless purity of the redeemed spirit is a truth that is supported by scripture; yet, it has escaped much of the body of Christ. By understanding its implications, we can deal with the real source of besetting sin, which is lodged in our soul (mind, will and emotions) and in our body. For even while our spirits are pure, our soul and body can be captured by sin.

DIVIDING BETWEEN SPIRIT, SOUL AND BODY

Your spirit is that part of you that enables you to know God and contains your moral nature (your conscience). Jesus said, "*God is a spirit, and those who worship Him must worship in spirit and in truth* (John 4:24)." You cannot know God in your mind, emotions, or body. Only your spirit can know God.

Our souls consist of our intellect, emotions and will. We live in our soulish realm through thoughts, emotions, and choices. Both your soul and spirit are eternal and will live forever, while your body is temporal and returns to the dust of the earth at death.

At conversion, it is the spirit – and only the spirit – that becomes new. We have the same body, mind, will and emotions as before. Every Christian has had the rude awakening that sinful and selfish attitudes

2

did not suddenly disappear. We become sin-conscious because we dwell mostly in the realm of the soul and **our souls have not been born again.** It is only our spirits that take on a new nature when we are born again.

Before we are born again, our entire being (spirit, soul, and body) was totally corrupted by sin. No matter how good or righteous our deeds or motives appeared to us or others, they were as "filthy rags" before God because they emanated from corruption.

"For all of us have become like one who is unclean, and all our righteous deeds are like a filthy garment; and all of us wither like a leaf, and our iniquities, like the wind, take us away." (Isaiah 64:6)

Romans 6:6 declares that when we were born again "our body of sin" was "done away with that we should no longer be slaves to sin."

"Knowing this, that our old self was crucified with Him, that our body of sin might be done away with, that we should no longer be slaves to sin."
(Romans 6:6)

This body of sin was totally expelled, not from the physical body, but from the spirit.

OUR RECREATED SPIRIT

After conversion, the only thing that can possibly emanate from the spirit is that which is of the nature of Jesus.

"No one who is born of God practices sin, because His seed abides in him; and he cannot sin because he is born of God." (I John 3:9)

This verse refers to the recreated spirit, which cannot sin because it is born of God and impregnated with the seed of Jesus Christ. If this verse referred to the soul, the Christian would fall prey to either great pride or great condemnation. He would have to conclude that either he now never sins, or that because he sins, he must not be born again. This is the trap that many get into through failing to divide between soul and spirit.

So, after you are born again, your recreated spirit is free from sin and contains only the nature of Jesus. However, within your flesh is still resident the corruption of sin. You soul can be dominated either by your recreated spirit, in which is resident the Holy Spirit, or by your flesh, in which is resident sin.

THE BATTLE FOR THE SOUL

When you are born again, a battle ensues between your spirit and your flesh for control of your

soul. **Whenever, and in whatever areas your spirit reigns over your soul, you manifest the nature of Jesus, and conversely, when and where your flesh dominates your soul, you manifest the nature of sin.** This is why true, born again Christians sometimes live like Jesus, and sometimes live like the devil.

Galatians 5:16–17 states that our spirit and flesh are at odds with each other for control of our will.

> *"But I say, walk by the Spirit, and you will not carry out the desire of the flesh. For the flesh sets its desire against the Spirit, and the Spirit against the flesh; for these are in opposition to one another, so that you may not do the things that you please."*
> *(Galatians 5:16 – 17) NAS*

Verse 16 states that if we walk in the spirit, we **will not** carry out the desire of the flesh. Many have taken this to mean that walking in the spirit means not doing the will of the flesh. Therefore, they **try** not to do the will of the flesh and thereby think that they are walking in the spirit.

However, Paul is not admonishing us to try not to walk in the flesh. He is telling us that if we allow our souls to be dominated by our recreated spirits, we **will not** (cannot, it is impossible) do the will of the flesh. Because there is nothing in the born again spirit except the nature of Jesus Christ, if the spirit dominates the soul, the Holy Spirit manifests His nature and sin cannot fulfill the will of the flesh.

Deep inside each of us is an underlying belief that we can really control our thoughts and behavior through "will power." I Peter 1:16 tells us, *"You shall be holy, for I am holy."* We have interpreted that to mean we should **try** to be holy in our thoughts and actions because God is holy, and He wants us to be holy. But this is not an admonition; rather it is a statement of fact. The believer already is holy, because God is holy and it is His nature that is in the regenerated spirit. This is the truth of whom I already am in my spirit. Whenever I allow my spirit to reign in my soul, holiness is automatically manifest in my life.

In John 14:15, Jesus said, *"If you love Me, you will keep My commandments."* We have assumed He meant that we should try to keep His commandments so as to prove our love for Him. Again, this is not an admonition, but a statement of fact. *"If you love me, you will (because of My nature in your spirit) keep My commandments."*

We cannot "keep His commandments" or "be holy" or avoid doing the "will of the flesh" by willpower. If we could, God would not have wasted the precious Blood of Jesus. He would have simply sent teachers and encouragers to show us how to **control** sin. However, God knew that it would never be possible to deal with sin in man except by recreating his spirit devoid of sin through the power of the shed Blood of Jesus. We are not called to **control** sin, but to die to it!

If we abide in Him, in His love, walk in the spirit, we will not and even cannot sin. When your

6

mind, will and emotions are yielded to your born again spirit, you **will** walk in the nature of Jesus. This is what the Bible means by walking in the Spirit. So, in order to walk in righteousness and holiness, all we have to do is yield our souls to our recreated spirits and walk in the spirit.

WALKING IN THE SPIRIT

This sounds so simple. But why then do we continue to experience ourselves walking in the flesh? For most Christians, the problem is not lack of desire. Not many of us **plan** to walk in the flesh. Most of us sincerely want to serve God. We never get up in the morning and consciously say, "I think I will walk in the flesh today!" However, sin in our flesh rises up through deception and captures the soul.

The primary deceptive tool Satan uses is to cause us to self-identify with sin. When we recognize our flesh controlling in some area of our lives, we then agree with the devil that this is our true identity. We are led to identify ourselves according to our flesh rather than according to our true nature in the spirit. We say, "I am just a critical person," or "I am frequently depressed," or "I have always been prone to lust," or "That is just my temperament."

Paul tells us in II Corinthians 5:16 that we now recognize **no man** according the flesh.

Therefore from now on we recognize no one according to the flesh; even though we have known Christ according to the flesh, yet now we know Him in this way no longer. (II Corinthians 5:16) NAS

It is this identifying of ourselves in the Spirit and not according to the flesh, even when the flesh is currently manifesting itself in our behavior, that Apostle Paul speaks about in Romans 7:10 – 14. In this passage, Paul describes the battle in his soul between what his recreated spirit wishes to do and what his flesh compels him to do.

"But if I am doing the very thing I do not wish I am no longer the one doing it, but sin which dwells in me." (Romans 7:20) NAS

Here Paul has disassociated his personal identity (I, the spirit man, **who wishes**), from sin in his flesh (I, the soul man captured by the flesh, **who does**).

In this passage, Paul uses the word "I" many times, but is actually describing different parts of his being. Below I have written the passage with each "I" amplified to describe which part of his being I believe Paul is speaking about.

For that which I, **(the soul), am doing, I, **(the spirit)**, do not understand; for I, **(the soul)**, am not practicing what I **(the spirit)**, would like to do but I, **(the soul)**, do the very thing I, **(the spirit)**,do not wish to do, I **(the spirit)**, agree with the Law, confessing that*

8

*it is good. So now no longer am I, (**the spirit**), the one doing it, but sin which indwells me, (**in my flesh**). For I, (**the spirit**), know that nothing good dwells in me, that is, in my flesh; for the wishing is present in me, (**the spirit and the soul together**), but the doing of the good, (**in the soul**), is not. For the good that I, (**the spirit and the soul together**), wish, I, (**the soul**), do not do; but I, (**the soul**), practice the very evil that I, (**the spirit and the soul together**), do not wish. But if I, (**the soul**), am doing the very thing I, (**the spirit and the soul together**), do not wish, I (**the spirit**), am no longer the one doing it, but sin which dwells in me, (**in my flesh**)." (Romans 7:15- 20)* * bold words are the author's

In disassociating his personal identity from sin in his flesh, Apostle Paul is viewing sin, in a sense, almost as something external to himself; like the unauthorized invasion of a foreign object. If a particle of dust flies into my eye, I would never identify myself with it. I would not say that it was a part of me. I would not simply accept blurred vision and watering eyes as "the way vision is for me." No! Of course not! I would regard the particle of dust as a foreign object that has invaded my physical body without authorization, and I would immediately take measures to remove it.

I am not saying that we are absolved from responsibility when sin manifests through us. Unlike a particle of dust entering the eye, sin does pass through our will and we do make a conscious choice to let it operate, albeit most of the time it is through

deception. Nonetheless we are responsible for the choices we make.

> *"The soul* (not spirit) *who sins will die."*
> *(Ezekiel 18:4) NAS*

However, there are two very important reasons why we should not identify ourselves with sin in our flesh.

1) The Bible tells us that we should have God's attitude toward sin. We then quickly discover that God's attitude toward sin is hatred. It is an abomination to Him. If I must have God's attitude toward sin, then I must hate it too Now, if I identify myself with sin operating through my flesh, and I believe that sin is "me," then whom must I hate? Myself, of course. When you hate yourself you feel very ashamed and disappointed in yourself, and you usually believe that God feels about you the same that you feel about yourself. Then you won't run to Him in repentance or receive His forgiveness and let Him set you free. Instead, you try to stop the sin yourself, so that you can then come to God without shame and feel right before Him. You then fail all the more, because you don't have the power to stop it, and you have through fear and shame cut yourself off from the only One who has power to deliver you. The more you fail, the more you identify yourself with the sin, and become convinced that it really is you and will never change.

2) When sin manifests through your soul, it is the fruit of your flesh. In every piece of fruit are many seeds. When you identify sin in your flesh as being "you," you plant that fruit and all the seed within it in the soil of your soul. If there are 10 seeds in the fruit, and each seed produces a tree bearing 100 new pieces of fruit, you can very quickly see a 1,000 fold multiplication of that kind of fruit in your life.

"Do not be deceived. God is not mocked; for whatever a man sows, this he will also reap. For the one who sows to his own flesh shall from the flesh reap corruption, but the one who sows to the Spirit shall from the Spirit reap eternal life."
(Galatians 6:7-8) NKJV

So we see that when we disassociate our personal identity from sin in our flesh, we are free to have God's attitude toward sin and toward ourselves. I can hate sin without hating myself and thus be free to run to my Heavenly Father and let Him love me and set me free. If after repenting and receiving forgiveness I then identify myself with the true nature of my recreated spirit, *"Christ in me, the hope of glory"* (Colossians 1:27), I am then nullifying the fruit of my flesh and sowing the fruit of my recreated spirit into my soul. Some time ago, the Holy Spirit convicted me of often making critical, sarcastic remarks toward others. Usually, my humor was at the expense of another person. The Lord showed me that this behavior was not emanating from His nature in my spirit, but

rather from my flesh, and was hurting others whom I had no conscious intention of hurting. I decided to begin guarding my words carefully so as not to hurt others.

Over the next few days, I watched my words with great diligence. However, a few unkind comments slipped out anyway and I was convicted of them after the fact. I was discouraged by these defeats, but decided to redouble my efforts. Over the next few days, I still did not recognize many of these comments until after they were out of my mouth. It seemed that the more I tried to stop these comments, the more I was defeated. Realizing my own inability to rid myself of sin working through me, I pleaded with God to take those thoughts and comments away from me. However, it did not seem that God was helping me. I began to feel abandoned by the Lord. I was doing everything I knew to do, and wasn't having victory. The more I tried, the more conscious I became of how miserably I was failing and the more condemned I felt. I thought to myself, "I will never get rid of this. It's just the way I am. I am a critical and sarcastic person." Finally, I heard the Holy Spirit say, "You are agreeing with the devil rather than with God about yourself. Your true nature in your spirit is not critical and sarcastic. I have already delivered you from that in your spirit. You are trying so hard to fight against sin in your mind, by which, you are trying to deliver yourself. It is not working."

The more I had tried to stop hurtful comments, the more conscious I became of my inability to do so.

If I tried harder, I only became more discouraged due to failure. I became angry at God because I couldn't obey Him and He would not help me. This process only served to deepen my identity with the flesh. Paul tells us in Romans 7:22–23 that any standard of behavior used as a law in the mind to attempt to overcome sin will always result only in failure and greater bondage.

*"For I joyfully concur with the law of God in the inner man, but I see a different law in the members of my body, waging war against **the law of my mind**, and making me a prisoner of the law of sin which is in my members." (Romans 7:22- 23) NAS*

When I recognized this, I repented of accusing God of not helping me (when He had already supernaturally recreated my spirit with the nature of Jesus Christ). I repented of identifying myself in the flesh and began to confess the truth of who I already was in the spirit. As I ceased concentrating on my words and started concentrating on Jesus, I allowed my spirit to reign in my mind, will and emotions. The more my spirit reigned, the more my mind was renewed and conformed to my true nature. Consequently, my words began to reflect the nature of my spirit. Instead of trying to **not** walk in the flesh, I began walking in the spirit. I then began to experience more and more victory over critical comments by simply letting my spirit reign in my soul.

13

So you can see that if you are always thinking of yourself as in the process of being conformed to the image of Christ, you never will be because you are identifying yourself with your flesh. If instead, you identify yourself with the nature of Christ already resident in your recreated spirit, you are sowing seed of the spirit into your soul. The scripture does not say, "If anyone is in Christ, he *will be* a new creation." It says, "*If anyone is in Christ, he is a new creation.*" (II Corinthians 5:17 NKJV) If you have committed your life to Jesus Christ, and have been born again, you are a new creation and as you begin to identify yourself as such, you will see more and more of the manifestation of Christ in your life.

Perhaps you have never received your Heavenly Father's offer to recreate your spirit by the power of the shed blood of Jesus Christ. If not, you may do so right now by simply praying a prayer as follows:

"Father God, I confess that I have sinned and I want to be born again through Your Son, Jesus. I now turn from my sin and ask You to forgive me. I believe in my heart that Jesus died for me, rose from the dead and now lives. Recreate my spirit, Lord, by the power of Jesus' shed blood. I receive Your cleansing and healing now. Thank you, Lord for my salvation, in Jesus name. Amen."

Mission/Vision of Family Foundations

<u>Mission Statement</u>: Equipping generations to find their identity and fulfill their destiny in Christ.
<u>Vision Statement</u>: To envision, impassion and mobilize the body of Christ to deliver to Jesus His inheritance in the saints through the restoration of God's ancient paths.

Who should come to The Ancient Paths Seminar?

Anyone desirous of lasting change in his/her life. Many times we see unpleasant or unhealthy patterns in our lives, but we don't know why they are there and/or can't seem to change. This ministry is designed to identify the root causes and bring lasting change to these areas.

For a schedule of future seminars or for information on how your church can schedule The Ancient Paths Seminar, please call or contact us on the World Wide Web.

(303) 797 – 1139

www.familyfi.org

You won't want to miss Family Foundations International

ANCIENT PATHS SEMINAR

<u>What Is It?</u> An intensive time of teaching from God's word, followed by sharing, prayer, and ministry in small groups. As teaching topics are brought up, the small groups give opportunity for ministry in that specific area of the individual's life, marriage, or family. The seminar is conducted in a Thursday evening, Friday evening, and all day Saturday format.

<u>Topics include</u>

Communication

- *Recognizing different levels of communication.*
- *Resolving Conflicts.*

Purpose and Plan
Identity and Destiny
Cursing and Blessing

- *Overview of God's plan and purposes for the individual and family.*
- *Seven Critical Times of Blessing.*
- *Releasing God's Blessing.*
- *Practical steps to freedom from cursing.*
- *Personal Ministry.*

Other Books by Craig Hill:

THE ANCIENT PATHS
BAR BARAKAH (A Parents Guide to a Christian Bar Mitzvah)
BONDAGE BROKEN
DECEIVED, WHO ME?
HELP! MY SPOUSE WANTS OUT
LIVING ON THE THIRD RIVER
MARRIAGE: COVENANT OR CONTRACT
WEALTH, RICHES & MONEY

For a current catalog of books and tapes by Craig Hill and other Family Foundations authors and speakers, please write:

Family Foundations International
P.O. Bo x 320
Littleton, CO 80160
www.familyfi.org

A list of Family Foundations Office around the world can be found on the website.